A VERY FOGG

JO EDWARDS

Published by Weasel Green Press

A VERY FOGGY CHRISTMAS

Cover Art by Carey Abbott
Edited by Mike Rose-Steel
Interior Text Design by Richard Edwards

ISBN: 978-1-908212-22-1

First Edition:

10 9 8 7 6 5 4 3 2 1

For Seaweed

Profile: Morten Astley Fogarty
Born: 22.11.1988
Works: (updated!) Customer Concerns
Advisor at Perypils Insurance & Front of
House/Barista at Smokey Joe's Bistro
Lives: Shodsworth, Gloucester
In a relationship with: Myra
Likes: Katy Perry, Taylor Swift, Shodsworth
Amateur Dramatic Society and Victoria
Pendleton's hybrid Halford's range

Simply Wizard

The nights were drawing in and I nearly rode straight into Mr Riddler as he hurried out of the park gates. Wrapped up in his long black raincoat, he was almost invisible against the dark sky, although I did think the evening a little too mild to warrant such a thick balaclava. Luckily, I spotted the whites of his eyes at the very last moment and managed to swerve round him. I'd taken care to wear my reflective, hi-viz cycling clips over my grey unisex waterproof-coated trousers - proof that you can dress sensibly and still look stylish.

Now it was dark, I had to take extra care arriving home as it was becoming increasingly difficult to spot the debris thrown onto our drive by mad Mrs Ryder who lived next door. Every time she saw Mum leaving the house, she'd fling open her kitchen window and pelt Mum with the contents of her waste bin. She'd scream with laughter while doing it: "HAW! HAW! HAW!" It was most distressing and I felt so sorry for the kindly Mr Ryder, who always used to be slipping in and out of ours, tool in hand, ready to tinker with something for Mum. Now, we didn't see him at all; I assumed he had to spend all his time caring for his poor wife. I didn't mind the tea bags and potato peelings so much, but the vodka bottles shocked me - she really should be recycling those.

Mum was washing her hands following another of her cake-making lessons. I was so proud of her for going self-employed and striking out on her own; she'd set up her business 'Over The Kitchen Table' when her Job Seekers had finally run out. It was early days, so money was still incredibly tight but who'd have thought - both my parents were now entrepreneurs! According to Auntie Trisha, Dad was a merchant banker, however he seemed to be involved in the car industry too; I'd received a letter from him stamped "HMP Ford". He really could turn his hand to anything and he must be doing incredibly well if he was in a High Management Position already.

"Who came today?" I asked Mum, picking a piece of squashed tomato off the sole of my trainer.

"Mr Grub. Very messy he was, too."

"What did you make?"

"Er, mince pies, but they won't be any good, his hands are far too cold for decent pastry."

"Were there any left over?" I asked hopefully, looking round.

"No, sorry son, and I haven't had time to go shopping so there's nothing for tea. Perhaps you could get some chips or something."

"That's ok, I've got a SADS meeting tonight - they're going to be announcing the lead roles for the Christmas production, I'm ever so excited!"

"I thought Myra said the auditions hadn't gone very well?"

"Oh, she only knocked me over a couple of times. The Follow the Yellow Brick Road dance was really difficult; we had to link arms and criss-cross our legs over each other's, which was a bit tricky because Myra had her spiked Doc Martens on. But all was good when my nose finally stopped bleeding, in fact, everyone said our vocals were unbelievable." I couldn't wait to get to the Jubilee Hall tonight to find out who had been awarded the lead parts - I had such a positive vibe about this one, everything felt right and my sciatica was so much better now, I could almost stand up straight. I'd only narrowly missed out on the role of Danny Zuko in Grease and although Frankie Trevino had been really good, he is a little too theatrical for The Wizard of Oz, which requires subtlety and panache. I badly want to play one of the main characters, and as everyone keeps telling me I have the perfect qualities to be the Scarecrow, my hopes are sky high.

My friends at work, Perypils Insurance, are extremely supportive of my singing and dancing, encouraging me to perform 'Ding Dong the Witch is Dead' when our Team Manager, Joy, goes to a meeting. They put their customers on mute and some of them even record me on their phones so they can promote me through Twitter and Facebook! I'm so lucky to have such wonderful colleagues and my new team is just as nice as my old one - when someone had to move departments to join Customer Complaints, my old team all voted for me! I was chuffed to bits at being chosen.

Admittedly, it's not the easiest job, as customers often call up in a distressed state, but I've only received three death threats so far, so I'm obviously doing something right.

I cycled to Myra's so I could give her a crossbar to the Jubilee Hall. Her mother opened the front door wearing a long blue dressing gown. "She's gone on ahead."

Aha; so Myra must be really excited too - she couldn't wait to get there! "No probs," I said. "I'll soon catch her up."

Her mother looked at me. "She's late, Foggy."

"Oh no, there's plenty of time. The meeting doesn't start until seven thirty."

"No - I mean she's *late*, late."

"Right, well, I'd better hurry *hurry* then!" I laughed, but Myra's mother didn't seem in the mood for joviality, as she shook her head and closed the door without saying goodbye. Never mind, at least she seemed a bit better than she had done at the weekend, when she'd simply sat in the corner of the lounge with a shawl over her head. Myra and I were trying to watch the Emmerdale omnibus, but it was difficult to hear what was going on over the chanting.

There was a real buzz of excitement at the Jubilee Hall. The SADS stood around in tight little groups, some examining their phones, others shifting from foot to foot, eagerly anticipating the announcement of the roles. My stomach was beginning to churn and I felt somewhat light-headed. Better calm down! Lead actors had to keep a lid on their nerves; I bet the wonderful Leonardo DiCaprio didn't get all bilious and queasy, not even before his sex scene with Tilda Swinton. I looked around the hall but couldn't see Myra. I nodded to Frankie Trevino who snapped, "Fuck off, bender!" Such an artistic temperament - he does make me laugh!

"Do you know where Myra is?" I asked Thin Lizzie, who was standing at the edge of the group twisting a hanky around and around into knots.

"I can guess," she mumbled and dabbed at her watery eyes. Poor Lizzie, she was undoubtedly feeling the pressure, having been chosen to play Sandy in Grease, our previous production. I'd have a chat with her later about resilience; after all, I never let each disappointment get me down, not even after twelve years. Playing a lamp post in 'Singin' in the Rain' was just as important as the Gene Kelly role, that's what Tom the director told me. He said there would always be someone in the audience watching you, even if you're mostly obscured by a speaker.

Tom suddenly burst out of the props cupboard and, with a very flushed face, strode across the hall towards us. *This was it!* We were about to find out! Where on earth was Myra? She was going to miss Tom's big announcement. I rammed my hands into the pockets of my Millets fleece and crossed my fingers, feeling my heart beginning to race. *Please, please, please - this time, let it be me, please let it be me.* Tom went over to the notice board and thrust a drawing pin into a sheet of paper. "Meeting's cancelled," he growled. "Here's the roles and if you've got any complaints, tell them to someone who gives a shit. Rehearsals start next Tuesday, so if you can't make it, don't bother coming back again."

As the door swung shut behind Tom, I rushed to the notice board, eager to beat the stampede. Oh my God - Myra was to play Dorothy! She'd done it, she'd got a lead part! I was so proud of her; those extra acting lessons Tom had been giving her must have really paid off - what a shame she wasn't here to share this wonderful moment. I read anxiously down the list of names. The Scarecrow had gone to Headbanging Harvey; drat, I knew I should have grown my hair longer. But there was still the Lion... No. That was Frankie Trevino. I must be the Tin Man, then! Oh no. That had gone to Nervous Noel. My name wasn't there! I fearfully scanned the list again. But no, I wasn't even a munchkin. Or a flying monkey. Even my mate Barry had been given a part, albeit Auntie Em, and he never even turned up to audition. How could I have been missed out? How?

I turned from the board in despair and saw Myra standing at the back of the hall, reading something on her iPhone. I hadn't seen her come in. I wanted to cry, but I knew I had to be strong and not spoil her joy. Swallowing hard to keep back the tears, I called, "Myra! Where have you been? You'll never guess what role you've got! You're only Dorothy!"

"Oh yeah," Myra was still texting.

"You mean, you already knew?" I asked, astonished.

"Er, no, I meant, oh yeah, that's great. I sort of expected it, to be honest. I mean, Tom knows I give the best performance in this group." She said this rather loudly, just as Thin Lizzie turned away from the board. "Oh hello Lizzie, I didn't see you there. Bad luck on not getting the lead this time round, but you know what Tom's like! He's no imagination, has he? Always typecasting! So what role did you get?"

I looked back at the board; Thin Lizzie was the Wicked Witch of the West. She let out a whimper and rushed from the hall. "Oops!" exclaimed Myra, taking my arm. "Me and my big mouth! Shall we go and celebrate our good news? Den's Diner is doing a meal-deal - cheesy chips, jumbo chilli dog and a coke all for £2.99! I'll have to have diet coke of course, as I'm being really careful with my calories."

"Yes, sure," I said, trying to stay upbeat. "Although I'm afraid I don't have any good news to celebrate myself."

"Oh, you'll make a great wizard!" cried Myra, punching my other arm. "You can put a spell on the cowardly-arsed lion and turn him into the greasy little rat boy that he really is." Frankie Trevino eyed us from the corner of the hall.

"What do you mean?" I asked, my left arm completely dead.

"You know, you're the Wizard!" I looked at her blankly. "The Wizard of Oz, dummy! Honestly Foggy, what did you think when we auditioned to The Merry Old Land of Oz? That we were doing Crocodile Dundee?"

I swung round to look at the board. There, handwritten right at the top of the piece of A4 paper, just under "The SADS proudly announce" was my name! The Wizard of Oz = Morten Fogarty. I hadn't thought to look at the very top of the page! It had happened, it had actually happened! I had been cast in a lead role at last! I think my legs would have collapsed if Myra hadn't been holding me up and propelling me out of the hall. I pedalled to Den's on cloud nine; only one arm had any feeling and Myra was buckling my cross bar, but it didn't matter. I knew my moment would finally come - if you wished for something hard enough, you could actually make it come true. I remembered Dad telling me that once when I was a little boy, just before he'd left me on my extendable toddler reins outside Ladbrokes. He had kept hold of my reins, of course, poking them through Ladbrokes's letter box so he could still shut the door behind him - he was a very conscientious father. Just think how proud he'd be to learn that his son had a lead role at last! As soon as I got home, I wrote a letter to Dad at the PO Box address I had for him. It was impossible to get to sleep - I was far too 'psyched', as my mate Barry would say, usually after he's been to the adhesives section at Homebase.

I cycled to work singing Queen's 'Don't Stop Me Now' between burps. The chilli dog was repeating on me very badly and I had the most dreadful wind; I felt so sorry for the paper-boy who was pedalling behind me. I couldn't wait to tell everyone in the office my news, but Joy, my team manager, stood over me until I put my headset on and logged into my telephone turret. I didn't even have time to look at my Internet banking or check Facebook like I normally would as part of my daily working routine. I was dying to tell her, but I didn't want to appear too boastful.

"Did you get up to much last night, Joy?"

"I watched Schindler's List again."

"Oh, how nice. Do you want to know what I did?"

"No. Where's your process maps, Morten? Why aren't they out on your desk?"

"Um," I rummaged around in my drawer. "I haven't seen them for a while, actually. I may have lent them to someone-"

"You must *always* have your process maps in front of you. Use them for every call. Here, take Tim's for now, and you'll have to find your own maps in your break."

Perypils were meticulous in their detail, with every single process mapped out in sophisticated flow diagrams. All you had to do was follow the arrows; it was impossible to go wrong. My first call of the day was from Mrs Drake, who was complaining because we'd denied her claim to cover a stay in a Bupa hospital. "Righto, just bear with me, Mrs Drake." I flipped through the process maps until I found one headed 'Healthcover - claim denied'. "Ok, here we go. So why was your claim rejected?"

"Why are you asking me? You sent me the bloody letter - haven't you got that information in front of you?"

"I can't flick through all these maps and use the computer at the same time you see, Mrs Drake. What did our letter say?"

"It said you wouldn't pay my hospital fees because I hadn't pre-authorised my stay."

"Oh dear. Did you forget?"

"No, I didn't forget, I was in labour. Funnily enough, when the contractions started, I didn't think to call my insurance company."

"Right." I looked closely at the process map. It read: 'Did customer pre-authorise treatment?' The choices were 'Yes' or 'No'. I followed the path for 'No', which was a long arrow down to the bottom of the page, ending in a red bubble with 'Reject complaint' written in it. "Um, I'm afraid you should have pre-authorised your treatment, Mrs Drake-"

"How could I pre-authorise it? And when, exactly? When I was being rushed into hospital in the ambulance? When I was screaming in agony in the delivery room? Or perhaps when I was being given an emergency C-section?"

"I'm sorry Mrs Drake, but my map says I can't accept your complaint."

"Your map? What are you talking about? And why have you sent my son a bill for £630 for his stay at the hospital?"

"Er, perhaps he forgot to pre-authorise too-"

"He'd only just been born! How the hell could he pre-authorise? Was he supposed to call you from inside my womb?"

I rifled through the maps but couldn't find one that covered pre-borns. "I haven't got a map for that complaint, Mrs Drake."

"What do you mean? For Christ's sake, it's like talking to a half-wit! I'd get more sense out of a fence panel. What the bloody hell does Perypils think it's playing at, you're a complete *disgrace-*"

I popped Mrs Drake on mute; letting customers vent their frustration was a very important part of Perypils' complaints handling policy, and it also gave me the opportunity to email everyone in the team to tell them my fantastic news. Sky, who sat opposite me, emailed back to say she had sensed a very strong aura around me this morning and I beamed at her over our blue soundboard. Her real name was Sheila, but she said Sky was her 'earth' name. Sky was just brilliant with our customers, so calm and soothing, expertly using open questioning techniques: "What do you expect me to do about it?" or providing clarification when required: "It's really not my problem". She was just perfect in a complaint-handling role and she didn't even need to use the process maps anymore, or "those fascist mind-restrictors" as she jokingly referred to them.

The morning passed very quickly as I was in such high spirits, having a great time chatting away with my customers. A couple of times, I had to place them on hold and nip to the loo at top speed but it was only wind, so I made it back before the callers noticed I'd gone. My mate Barry always says "never trust a fart". I must remind him that he still owed me £12 for the jogging bottoms I'd had to buy for him in Tesco's.

As I ended my call with a Miss Turner, after she'd eventually stopped sobbing, I realised Joy was standing beside me. She was a very slender lady and it was difficult to see her when she was side-on. "Hello Joy," I began, "Did I tell you my news? I'm-"

"What have you done now, Morten?"

"I got the lead part in the SADS Christmas production!"

"I meant, what have you done wrong? Kate wants to see you."

My bowels twinged and a small guff of wind escaped. "I, er, I haven't done anything wrong." Why should Kate want to see me? Oh, but of course - good news travelled fast in this office. I beamed. "I expect she wants to congratulate me, Joy. You know what a keen interest she takes in our personal lives and our hobbies outside of work. I bet she's dead chuffed for me."

Joy was looking rather pained - perhaps she'd had the meal deal at Den's Diner too. "You haven't tried to sell motor insurance to a blind person again, have you, Morten? And what about Mr Dogetard - have you upset him recently? Don't tell me you've mispronounced his name again."

"Oh no, I don't think so-"

"Come on, she's waiting. And for goodness sake, empty your bin. There's a terrible smell round here."

Kate, our department manager, was sitting at her desk in the corner of the room and was clearly deep in thought, holding her head in her hands. It must be such a demanding job, running two departments, but Kate was always so good-humoured and chirpy - I didn't know how she managed it. Joy cleared her throat and Kate looked up at us through her fingers. "Ah, Morten," she sighed, lowering her hands and moving a packet of Nurofen to one side. "I've got a little test for you."

"Oh great, I love quizzes! Is it on Christmas songs from the eighties? My mum's playing them all the time at the moment - I think I could sing every single one of them."

"Not with a hole punch lodged in your throat, you couldn't!" Kate's left eye twitched, and I winked back at her - she was always so playful. She rubbed a hand across her forehead. "Right Morten, first question. Which department do you work in?"

Too easy! "Customer Complaints," I said, emphatically.

"No, it's Customer Concerns."

"Oh, right; has the name recently changed?" Beside me, I sensed Joy flinch.

Kate tapped her fingernails on the desk. "Yes, Morten, it *recently* changed about six months ago. Let's try an easier one, shall we? What is the point of you?"

"Sorry?"

"What do you see as the main purpose of your role?"

"Well," I thought for a moment. "It's to help customers with their complaints." A bony elbow jabbed my ribcage. "Ow! Er, I mean, with their concerns."

"And when you say help them with their concerns, can you define what you mean by 'help'?"

"Um, resolve their concern."

"YES!" Kate shrieked, making us jump. Thank goodness - I'd got that one right. "*Resolve* their concern! As in, sort out their problem, put it right, send them away happy. What we try really hard *not* to do, Morten, is give them further cause for complaint. So, with that in mind, can you tell me why I've just had to spend the last forty minutes pacifying Mr Harris?"

"Oh, that's a coincidence! I spoke to a Mr Harris this morning, too."

"Yes, you did, Morten. And can you remember what you said to him?"

"Um, I think he was complaining, I mean, concerning, about his claim taking too long... Yes, that's right. I transferred him to Claims."

Kate was tapping again. "Did you say anything else? Something a little out of the ordinary for an insurance helpdesk, maybe?"

I racked my brains. "I don't think so."

"Because he told me you'd propositioned him." Beside me, Joy emitted a squeak. "Apparently, you said to him-," Kate paused and picked up her note-pad, "I'm like a sex machine that's ready to re-load, and I'm having a ball. So if you want to have a good time, please give me a call."

"Oh, how funny – I've had a song in my head all morning and I must have been voicing the lyrics! But he got them wrong, you know, it should be-"

"Never mind the sodding lyrics, Foggy!" I noticed Kate's knuckles turn white as she gripped her hole-punch and Joy dodged behind me. Kate took a deep breath, released the hole-punch and pinged a pink elastic band that was round her wrist. Ouch! She looked at me. "Morten - I do understand that with one song in your head there's not much room for anything else, but do you think you could try and limit your conversations with our customers to questions relating to their policies?"

"I thought I'd put Mr Harris on hold."

"You keep muddling up hold and transfer," chipped in Joy. "I've told you about a hundred times."

"I think the team swap the buttons around on my telephone turret," I explained. "They're always doing little things like that to cheer me up! Such a great bunch, aren't they? Only yesterday they re-arranged the letters D, K, I and C on my keyboard when I'd gone to lunch. They do make me laugh!"

I could have chatted to Kate all day; she was such fun, but she clearly needed a wee as she'd started rocking backwards and forwards, and Joy pulled at my sleeve, saying we ought to leave her in peace. I didn't get to tell Kate about the Wizard of Oz! I sent her an email when I was back at my desk, and offered to reserve a front row seat for her – I couldn't wait to see her face when she discovered *that* in her inbox!

the floor. "You're not doing that mumbo jumbo Typhoo shite, are you Mum? I thought you'd stopped seeing elephants in ink blots."

"But it's a sign, Myra, a clear sign!"

"A sign that you're about to be sectioned?"

"No, it's a sign for you - there's a penis in my saucer, Myra, and that hasn't happened since your father left me for that tranny-looking thing. Don't you see what this means?"

"No."

"It means it's a boy, it's definitely a boy."

I looked from one of them to the other; Myra had flushed dark red. "Oh, thanks a bunch, Mum!" she spat. "I haven't had the chance to tell him and now you've just gone and blabbed it out! Well done, I hope you're proud of yourself, you gormless retarded old trout."

"He deserves to know. How long were you planning on keeping him in the dark? It's not fair."

What on earth were they talking about? I often found girly chatter rather difficult to comprehend and it didn't help that I'd obviously walked in on a private conversation. I felt I had to break the awkward silence. "Shall we go to your room and rehearse, Myra?" I asked, hopefully. "I could take the part of the Scarecrow if you want to practise 'If I Only Had a Brain'."

They both stared at me for a moment, then Myra got up and rushed out. I heard the door to the downstairs cloakroom slam shut again. Poor thing, this hay fever was really affecting her. Never mind, I'd just have to go home and practise on my own, unless Mum had one of her heads, of course - if so, I'd mouth the words silently into the hallway mirror again.

After an extremely busy morning on the phones, I had lunch with my mate Barry, who was on a break from his community service. We went to Jabba's, which did a sausage and onion six-inch baguette for 99p. Barry, still in his waders, smelt strongly of stagnant water, so we had to go outside and sit on the wall with our baguettes, after a woman seated inside with a dribbly bulldog protested that we were unhygienic. "So, what have you been doing, Barry?"

"What d'yer think? They don't make you dress like this to serve afternoon tea at the Ritz, do they? Been clearing out Shit Creek again; found seventeen Asda trolleys in there this morning. And a Fiat Uno."

"Do they work you very hard?"

"Nah, the Gaffer's usually too stoned to notice what's going on. Jimmy can get all the way to Morrison's, nick some vodka, score some crack *and* make it back; he's never been missed."

"Are you coming to rehearsals tonight? Tom's pretty keen that all the cast attend."

Barry snorted. "You must be bloody joking, I don't want my hearing permanently damaged by your bird's foghorn. Size of her lungs, people will think the QE2's coming up the canal."

"She has got a wonderfully powerful voice, hasn't she?" I said, proudly. "I can't wait to hear her Over the Rainbow."

"Oh, they'll hear her over the rainbow, alright. Probably cause another Tsunami in Asia."

"I just hope she's ok, she hasn't been very well lately and it's made her a little bit, er, uptight, you could say."

"Turned psycho again, has she? I saw her coming out of the doctor's yesterday - testosterone reduction, was it? Or just getting her prostate checked?"

I laughed. I knew he liked Myra really; he always offered to walk her home when she'd had so much to drink she didn't know what was what or who was who and couldn't stay upright on my crossbar. But why hadn't Myra mentioned going to the doctor's? It must have been because of her terrible winter hay fever and she probably didn't want to worry me. I followed Barry back inside to get a can of coke and we played football with a Jabba-giant muffin while we waited in the queue for the counter. The frizzy-haired woman at the till shouted, "Oi! I hope you're going to pay for that!"

Barry looked horrified. "I'm not paying for that - it's been kicked all round the floor!"

I whizzed to the Jubilee Hall on my bike, feeling really buzzed up and ready to perform my socks off. I had prepared very thoroughly, running through my vocal exercises and gargling with onion and warm water for my adenoids. I used to gargle with onion, warm water and saliva, until Mum told me I'd misunderstood Google where it said "and spit". To think I'd been doing it wrong all these years! And it was only recently that I'd worked out you were supposed to use the juice from an onion and not the whole thing. I also did my stretches, which help my sciatica, so I would be all nice and loose for the dancing. One of Mum's clients was in the kitchen finishing his cigarette, and he tried to show me an exercise for my back. He said I should kneel down on all fours, then take my bottom very slowly backwards, brace myself and hold that position for about one minute forty-five seconds. He very kindly offered to crouch down behind me to keep me steady, but Mum came in and stopped us. She doesn't really like me fraternising with her clients – she's a real pro.

The SADS gathered at the Jubilee Hall were fizzing with anticipation as they always did when a new production was about to commence, it was a terrific atmosphere. I removed my purple folding cycling helmet and pushed open the door to the hall - I was entering as the lead actor! *What a moment.* I was delighted to see that Myra had made it. She was chatting to Tom and had dressed in her best outfit of leopard print tunic and black leather-look leggings. She'd even put on her special-edition Doc Martens that had flames all down the sides - what an authentic Dorothy she was going to make! The lovely Judy Garland herself could not fail to be impressed; perhaps we should invite her to the opening night.

Frankie Trevino slouched in the corner, hands stuffed into the pockets of his trendy designer jeans. A packet of Marlboro's poked out from the top pocket of his denim jacket. He always looked so cool, and I couldn't wait to see him all dressed up as the Cowardly Lion! He was going to be brilliant. I beamed over at him but he shouted: "What are you gawping at, bum bandit?" He did get a little tense before a performance and he probably felt a bit upset that he'd lost out on the lead to me. Funny how things were reversed this time round! My luck had certainly changed.

When Tom and Myra finally stopped talking, Tom called us together and said we were going to start with Dorothy's arrival in the Land of Oz and then into 'Follow the Yellow Brick Road'. I managed to grab a quick word with Myra as shittiest service imaginable! All these calls are costing me a bloody fortune."

"Oh dear, Mrs Stewart, I am sorry about that. But I am able to offer you some cunnilingus."

"*What?*"

"I'd like to give you cunnilingus." Silence. "Are you still there, Mrs Stewart?"

I couldn't actually hear her reply because she shrieked it so loudly I was temporarily deafened. I whipped my headset off and held it a couple of feet away from me, waiting until the screams subsided and my turret told me Mrs Stewart had hung up. Not a good start to the morning, but I did so want to win the half day's holiday. The flashing red screen above my head told me there were forty-seven in the queue, so I plugged straight back in, determined to satisfy the next customer.

I arrived at Smokey Joe's and turned on the lights, the heating and the coffee machine. Then made a start on the leftover washing-up from Saturday. Joe used to have a top-of-the-range dishwasher but he'd lost it on a game of Go Fish with the guys from Loch Fyne. Unusually, there was no sign of Joe this morning so I opened up, praying nobody came in for hot food until he'd arrived.

I tried to make myself a cappuccino, but the coffee machine had not fully woken up and squirted a pale, lukewarm liquid into my cup. I pressed the grinder and watched a small dark mound beginning to form as I hummed 'Another Rock n' Roll Christmas'. You didn't see much of Gary Glitter these days; I wonder what he's been up to? Probably sliding gracefully into old age with a loving wife at his side.

A sharp tap on my arm made me jump and I swung round to find a frozen-faced woman standing at the counter. Her eyes looked angry and she mouthed something at me. "Sorry, what was that?"

"I SAID, TURN THAT BLOODY THING OFF!"

"Oh yes, sorry." I flicked the grinder off and picked up my pad to take her order. She had a little girl with her and I smiled at both of them. "What can I get you?"

"I want some sandwiches to take away; do you think you can manage that, or do we have to stand here all day? What fillings do you have?"

"We have ham, cheese, tuna-"

"Smoked salmon?"

"Er, no-"

Mum had obviously ventured out today as the drive was littered with orange peel and used tea bags. I wheeled my bike carefully round the back and found my mother in the kitchen gulping out of her Trophy Wife pint mug. "Gosh Mum, you look thirsty! Have you just been giving someone another session? You'd better go easy or there won't be enough water left in the tap for our Pot Noodles!"

"It's not water," gasped Mum, wiping her mouth. "It's wine. Your grandmother's here. And I hope you don't need the bathroom, she's been in there for one hour forty five minutes."

"Oh dear, didn't the prune juice work? We had such high hopes for that, didn't we?"

"Nothing works; she's ninety percent cement."

"What was it you used to give me, when I was very little?"

"Strongbow. I'm not giving her cider though, not with her flatulence."

"Poor Gran. I hope she doesn't leave bite marks in the soap again."

I put the kettle on for a cup of tea and sank into a chair, grateful to sit down for the first time today. I heard the toilet flush and then shuffling footsteps in the passage. The hunched, dark figure of Granny Pattern appeared in the doorway. "Why don't you get some decent toilet paper, Pam?" she asked, huffily. "I get mine from the disabled loos in Debenhams; real good quality that is and the rolls are huge, but they still fit inside my wheelie trolley. Yours is like sandpaper! And so cheap and nasty, my fingers went right through it." She sat down gingerly and held out her hands to me. "Well, give your Grandma a kiss then, boy."

I leant across, trying not to shudder, taking her bony hand and kissing her whiskery cheek. "Would you like a cup of tea, Gran?"

She sniffed. "I reckon I need something stronger after all my exertions; fair wiped me out, it has. I need to build my strength back up - have you got a nip of brandy?"

"No," shot Mum. "You can have some cooking sherry, if there's any left, that is. I had to use quite a bit on the limescale round the bath."

The beady black eyes narrowed. "You always were a tight one, Pam, *always*. Don't think I haven't forgotten last Christmas, pretending that was a fresh turkey you got from the butchers. You didn't fool me! That tiny sliver of breast you served me was still partially frozen, despite all the boiling Bisto you tipped over it. I didn't bring you up to be so dishonest, Pam; I don't know where you get it from."

"Is it alright if Myra comes again this year?" I asked Mum. "Her mother doesn't really do Christmas; well, she told me she couldn't be arsed with it all."

"Yes, of course Myra can come."

"Just keep the Thornton's away from her this time," grumbled Granny Pattern. "Troughed her way through both layers last year, only left the toffee caramels, and they stuck my dentures together. You remember, Pam? I had to sit with my chin over a tea light for half an hour before they loosened up."

"Best thirty minutes of Christmas ever," muttered Mum, trying to shake the last drops out of the wine bottle with great determination. A little louder she said: "Auntie Trisha and Biffa will be here too, and I expect you to show a little more others who were pressed against the back of the hall, some with their hands covering their ears so they could channel the wonderful sound more effectively. Thin Lizzie clung onto the water jugs, the vibration causing them to move around on the top of the counter. Myra finished with a truly heart-rending "Why, oh why can't I?" and held the end note for a full twenty seconds, maintaining concentration even when two trestle tables collapsed around her. What a trooper!

Tom the director led the applause, swallowed a handful of Nurofen, then organised everyone for 'We're Off to See the Wizard'. Great - this must be where I come in! But no; it was just Dorothy and the Munchkins as they waved her off from Munchkinland, and then the same song again but with the Scarecrow, the Lion and the Tin Man. Whenever Tom was distracted or had his head in his hands, Frankie Trevino changed the lyrics to "If ever, oh ever, a spaz there was, the Wazzock of Oz is one because..." and gesticulated towards me with his flick knife. Did the Cowardly Lion carry a flick knife in the film version? I thought that was East Side Story.

Tom really put them through their paces, making Myra do the Yellow Brick Road dance in front of him over and over again. She was going to be exhausted, all that jumping up and down! She wasn't very happy about being pelted by apples by the Talking Tree, played by Trunky Tracy, and I thought the Wicked Witch a little over-zealous in her encouragement, yelling "Harder! In the face! Get her in the face!" but all in all, I think it went pretty well. I leapt up hopefully when they reached the Emerald City, but they didn't get to meet with the Wizard, instead skipping ahead to practise the flying monkeys' attack. I tried to speak to Tom at the end of rehearsals, but he swept past me and out of the hall before I could catch him. Myra would have left too if I hadn't called out to her. "Hi Myra!"

"Oh, hello Foggy, I didn't know you were here."

"Thought you would have smelt him," Frankie joked, pushing past Myra as he left the hall.

"Yes, thought I'd better come, in case I was required. I wasn't, as it goes ... I thought you were brilliant, by the way! Your solo was so moving - some of the cast actually had tears in their eyes! Shall we go to Den's - cheesy chips and curry sauce to celebrate?"

"Er, no, not tonight," Myra said, tugging at the door. "Got to, er, colour Mum's hair for her and you know how long that takes me, especially unblocking the plug hole afterwards."

"Oh, ok."

"See you tomorrow, though? Do some shopping?"

"Yes, shall I meet you-" I started, but she was gone. That was odd; I'd never known Myra turn down cheesy chips before. Perhaps she was trying extra hard with her diet this time – after all, she did appear to have put on a little more weight recently. I'd never say that to her, of course; the last person to do that had been impaled on a kebab skewer. I called out goodbye to the rest of the cast, who were having a chat over an orange squash, but they didn't hear me. I left the hall and went to unlock my bike. Oh no! Someone had carved 'TWAT' into my gel-sprung comfort saddle. The kids from the affordable housing estate, probably. Oh well, never mind; no doubt this was exactly how Darren Day had started his musical career and he'd never let little setbacks get him down - just look at him now! I pumped up my tyre again and cycled home.

I met Myra outside Evans, although she was almost an hour later than we'd arranged because she'd been sick again. Poor Myra was having a terrible time with her health just recently! I wondered if she could be suffering from stress. After all, living at home and not going to work could take its toll. Perhaps I should ask Sky for some relaxation techniques. I followed Myra around Evans but she seemed to be looking for clothes for herself rather than presents for others. "What do you think of this, Foggy?" she asked, holding up a voluminous black smock top.

Based on previous experiences, I knew I was in very dangerous territory. If I replied, "Yes, that's nice" I would be accused of "not giving a crap". If I replied, "I don't really like that one" I would be accused of "having the dress sense of Susan-sodding-Boyle". (Mind you, I'd seen a picture of Susan and I thought she looked rather charming in her purple polo neck jumper, tangerine jacket and zebra print fringed scarf.) I tried to respond in the helpful, kindly manner of Gok. "Er, I like the colour, it really suits your skin tone. I'm just wondering if it might be a little baggy on you." I peered at the label. "It says 'maternity', Myra."

"Um, what about this one, then?" She pulled out a jazzy, zig-zagged patterned tunic. My eyes went all swimmy.

"We're still in the maternity section though, aren't we? How about that lovely top over there? It's all sparkly - perfect for Christmas!"

I went over to the glittery section and examined the sequined top. "This is a great shape for you!" I said, playfully. "It will show off your beautiful bouncy bits to perfection!" I turned round, beaming, but found myself looking into the wizened face of a little old lady. She stared back at me, her mouth dropping open in horror. I thought Myra had followed behind me! But no, I could see she was still in the maternity section. Muttering "Sorry, sorry", I quickly left the shop. Best to wait outside.

Myra wanted to go to Smokey Joe's for lunch, thinking I'd get a staff discount, or "freebie" as she put it, but when we got there, we found it closed. I couldn't believe it - why on earth would it be closed? And on a Wednesday lunchtime, market day, when Joe hoovered up the over-spill from Greggs. I peered in the windows but there was no sign of Joe. *What a mystery.* We gave up and went to Burger King instead, where Myra felt well enough to order a double whopper with cheese and extra gherkins and their new gooey chocolate fudge bites. I said I was glad she'd got her appetite back and she replied, "Well, I'm eating for two", which I guessed meant this was her breakfast as well as her lunch. From the window, I saw a large man in a fifties-style suit passing by, the front of his hair gelled up into a tall quiff. He was holding the hand of a very slender lady, who turned and looked in our direction - it was Auntie Trisha! I waved like mad, and she spotted me, tugging her wife Biffa back towards Burger King.

"Wotcha Foggy!" Auntie Trisha exclaimed as they plonked themselves down at our table. "Blimey Myra, what the hell are those? Flame-grilled dog turds?"

"They're 'warm, bite-sized treats featuring a fudge-brownie outside and creamy molten chocolate filling on the inside'." Biffa read from the menu. "Can I try one?"

I looked anxiously at Myra; I didn't dare ask to share her food. Barry had tried to steal a chip once and almost had his hand severed. Myra, however, appeared unwilling to take on

Biffa, swallowing hard before eventually replying, "Yes, of course."

"Are you Christmas shopping too?" I asked them.

"Yes, isn't it the most bloody awful bind?" Auntie Trisha took a suck from my strawberry milkshake. "We literally couldn't move in Debenhams and in the end I had to machete my way through to reach Biffa's Eau Savage. But at least we've managed to find a great book for your Gran." She pulled a paperback from her Waterstones bag and handed it to me.

"Oranges Are Not the Only Fruit," I read. "Good idea to get her a book on fibre, given her dietary problems."

"Oh, this will give her the shits alright," Auntie Trisha grinned. "You ok there, Bifana?"

"Napalm," Biffa gasped, spluttering into a napkin. "It's stuck to the roof of my mouth."

"The turds are a bit on the warm side, aren't they?" Myra commented, a little smugly, I thought. We spooned the icy dregs of my milkshake onto Biffa's tongue until her eyes stopped watering.

"What do you want for Christmas, Foggy?" Auntie Trisha asked. "And don't say Halfords vouchers again, for Christ's sake, think of something original for a change. Something for you, not for running repairs on that bloody bike."

"Oh, er," *I really wanted Halfords vouchers!* "Perhaps a gift card then, from the Outdoor Warehouse-"

"Do they sell bicycle bollocks, by any chance?"

"Yes."

"Oh, for f-"

"Are you coming to see us in the Wizard of Oz on Boxing Day?" Myra asked them. "You know I'm playing Dorothy?"

"Is that officious little tit directing it again this year, you know, the one with the ridiculous door knocker beard?"

"Tom's an extremely talented director," Myra said, defensively. "And clearly an excellent judge of talent, seeing as he's cast me in the leading lady role."

"Has he tried you in many other positions, Myra?" Biffa slurred.

"We'd better let you crack on," cut in Auntie Trisha quickly, getting to her feet. "Lots to do and all that. See you both on Christmas Day; we'll bring stacks of booze, of course and some chloroform for your Gran. Shame we couldn't afford to send her to that clinic in Switzerland for Christmas, but still, we'll start saving for next year. See you!"

Myra and I didn't get much Christmas shopping done, in the end. Myra got into an argument with one of her old colleagues in Superdrug when she overheard her say "the facial hair remover is that way" and it all became very heated. Everyone was staring and I didn't know where to put my face, so I stood and examined the feminine hygiene products until the store manager came over and broke up the argument. Myra didn't feel like shopping after that, so we took the bus back to Shodsworth and I walked her home. She turned on the doorstep, looking very sad and said, "I've got something to tell you, Foggy."

"Oh dear, what is it? Did you get another rejection from Shipwrecked?"

"No, it's not that."

"Was it from The Voice, then? You mustn't be too downhearted you know, Myra - you've just got to keep trying! I thought your entry video was wonderful and I bet none of the other girls thought to sing a Barry White classic. Have you heard back from Big Brother yet?"

She sighed and shook her head, forgetting to say goodbye as she went into the house and shut the door. Poor Myra. I'd have to get her something extra special for Christmas to try and cheer her up a bit. I looked up 'Chucky: The Killer DVD Collection' on Amazon when I got home. It was a bit pricey but it was guaranteed to put a smile back on her face. That's the magic of Christmas!

Baby Talk

Myra hadn't felt like rehearsing, so I practised on my own, trying to perfect a powerful wizard's voice by booming into Mum's cooking funnel. She had called upstairs to ask me to stop at one point as she said it was putting her client off his stroke - they were having to do a lot of rolling, apparently. I had tried to make pastry once myself when we did sausage rolls in home economics, but Barry had accidentally knocked my oven temperature down and I don't think mine cooked properly. Mum, Dad and I were dashing in and out of the loo all night, with poor Dad having to squat over the drain in the garden when Mum took too a bit too long in the bathroom.

I arrived for work at Smokey Joe's on Sunday to find everything shiny and spotless; even the white dog poo had been removed from the doorstep. Joe was in the kitchen, chipping burnt bits of bread out of the toaster. "Morning Chef!" I called. "Are we having a winter spring clean?"

"Bloody health inspectors," Joe snarled, savagely hacking away with his screwdriver. "Been all over this place like a dose of the clap. Had to close for three whole days! Bleeding jobsworths; we never had this sort of shit at Claridges, Gordon just saw them off with a blow torch."

"Why did they come here?"

"Just because some anal busy body accused us of attempted murder. Attempted fucking murder! Hardly anyone dies of campylobacter these days. Some parents are so bloody over-protective - how does she even know it came from us? It can live in the body for bloody days! Probably had too much sushi at the fucking country club."

"It couldn't have come from us!" I exclaimed, astonished. "We've got a top hygiene rating - it says so on the board in the window."

"My mate Ron made that for me," said Joe. "He learnt all about computers and shit in Wandsworth. He's the one that writes our five star reviews on Tripadvisor."

"When are the inspectors coming back?"

"Tomorrow. So get your marigolds on and go and scrape that piss-paste off the toilet bowls. Use one of the steak knives. Shit!" He leapt backwards as a blue spark shot out of the toaster at him; he really should have unplugged it first.

I was absolutely exhausted by ten o'clock, scrubbing and wiping and polishing in between serving customers. Joe wanted every single utensil and piece of crockery cleaned, so I tried to reduce the workload by asking customers to share tea spoons and cake forks. Freckly Girl was very considerate, lifting her legs up out of the way with a friendly smile as I swept and Flashed the floors, not tutting and sighing like the other customers did.

Myra came in at twelve-thirty, when I should have been struggling with the lunchtime rush, but it was strangely quiet today. "What can I get you, Myra?" I asked, remembering Joe's instructions to push the prawns, which were past their sell-by. "A nice prawn and mayo baguette?"

"I can't have shellfish in my condition."

"Oh, are you constipated again? What about a piece of Joe's mushroom quiche, then? That should do the trick."

She sighed and rubbed her eyes. "I had a sausage and egg McMuffin at Maccy D's on my way here, so I'll just have a cheese toastie, I think. With extra pickle. And a piece of that chocolate fudge cake; just a small bit mind, I'm still being really careful. Can't you take a break for a minute? I need to talk to you."

I took her order through to Joe, who was down on all fours, his head and shoulders inside the large oven. That must take some cleaning! "Order for you, Chef!" I called cheerfully and went back to make Myra her cappuccino. I sat down opposite her and watched her suck the froth up through her teeth. "What did you want to talk about Myra, the rehearsals? I think they're going really well, apart from all the fisticuffs of course, but I'm sure-"

"No, it's not the rehearsals." She stirred her coffee and didn't look up. "It's something else. Something very important, Foggy. And you're not going to like it."

My stomach lurched. "What is it, Myra?" I asked in alarm. "Are you ill?"

"No, not ill exactly." She stopped stirring and looked up. "Can you smell gas?"

"Gas? No, I can't. It's probably bleach fumes, we've been using gallons of it."

"Oh, right. Well, look Foggy, there's just no easy way to tell you this." She took a deep breath and looked at me, her eyes all watery. What on earth was wrong? "I'm pregnant."

I gaped at her in astonishment. "Pregnant? You're *pregnant*? But, but, but, how? I mean, er, well, *how?*"

"The usual bloody way, Foggy! How do you think?"

"But we've always used two condoms!" I blurted. The little old lady sitting at the next table spluttered into her teacup. "You always make sure I'm double-bagged!"

"Yes." Myra was staring into her coffee again. "I do."

"Gosh." I sat back in my chair, totally stunned. A thought struck me and I put my hands to my face in horror. "Oh no! Oh no, no, no!"

She swallowed. "I'm really sorry, Foggy-"

"It's because I changed to Co-op's own brand, isn't it?"

"What?"

"Their own brand condoms! I thought I'd try and economise, you know; theirs work out at just nineteen pence a go, which I thought was really good-"

"Oh, for goodness sake, Foggy!"

"I'm so sorry Myra!" I clutched her hands. "It's all my fault! I should have known; Mum's always saying you get what you pay for - why didn't I listen to her? I could have cut back on Clearasil and got the more expensive condoms, you know, like the Mates blueberry muffin flavoured ones!"

"Foggy, I-"

"I should have been more careful!" I couldn't believe it - Myra was pregnant; I was going to be a father! And Mum was going to be a granny at last! She'd been dreading being the oldest grandmother out of her friends when she turned forty-five next year. But what a shock; if only Dad was here to advise me - what would he say to me right now? He'd say, "Gotta man up, son", just like he'd done when Rolo, my guinea pig, ran in front of the strimmer.

I squeezed Myra's hands reassuringly. "Don't you worry, Myra; don't you worry about a thing - I'm going to take care of you. Of both of you. I'll be here for you, every single step of the way. I'm going to stay right by your side; I'll never leave you, not for a moment."

Myra seemed lost for words and, overcome with emotion, burst into noisy sobs. I leapt up to fetch a napkin but before I could return to the table, she'd stumbled away into the toilets. Poor thing, her hormones must be all over the place. I'd heard about that sort of thing; Dad still bore the scars from when Mum was pregnant with me. He said she'd attacked him with an umbrella stand just because he hadn't wanted to leave the pub when her waters broke. He'd only just got a pint in, and it was his turn next on the pool table. Terrible things, hormones.

I was debating going into the Ladies after Myra, when the cafe was suddenly plunged into gloom as all the lights went out. The coffee machine gave a groan as it shuddered and went off too. Oh blimey - a power cut. "Sorry about this," I said to the old lady, who was peering into her pill box. I went to the kitchen to see how Joe would manage lunches without the microwave. He was still inside the oven and I could see that the dial was set to 'on'. Oh dear - he must have knocked it when he was cleaning. "Goodness me, Chef!" I exclaimed, turning the dial back to the 'off' position. "You're lucky we've had a power cut - you might have gassed yourself!"

Joe's reply was very muffled.

"What's that, Chef? You want me to go and do what?" I bent right down as he repeated it. "Hug myself? Well, that's very nice of you, Chef! I'll give myself a hug in just a minute. What shall we tell the customers - sandwiches only until we get the power back? The heating's gone off too, of course, so it's going to get a bit chilly." I couldn't resist telling him; I was bursting to tell someone! "Guess what, Chef? Myra's just told me she's pregnant - I'm going to be a Dad! Just think - there's a Mini Me on its way into the world!"

Joe stuck his left arm out of the oven and turned the dial back to 'on'. I laughed and started to fix Myra a healthy, nutritious salad. I knew she always said, "Do I look like a fucking tortoise?" when faced with anything leafy, but I wanted my child to have the best possible start in life. My child! It really was a miracle.

I was fizzing with excitement when I arrived at work on Monday morning. Myra had begged me not to tell anyone yet, but Mum caught me Googling 'baby bike seats' last night and had guessed straight away; she'd practically squealed the house down in her excitement, and had logged straight into the Direct Gov website to see what additional benefits we might be entitled to.

I'd written to Dad at the PO Box number I had for him in Manchester, imagining his face when he opened the letter; he'd be so thrilled! And he was bound to visit us now, no matter how difficult it was for him to take a break from all the business meetings that had kept him away for almost two years. He was going to be a terrific role model for my child.

"Morning Joy!" I called as I reached my desk, taking care to carefully pat my fingers around the work surfaces, checking for super glue. There was still a pair of my cycling clips stuck to the desk; I'd never been able to shift them. "What did you get up to at the weekend, go anywhere nice?"

"No." She stood up and came over to me, her face grey and creased. "I was here all weekend, with Kate. We were trying to, er, assemble some statistics for the auditors. I've been updating the concerns database for twelve hours solid."

"Oh yes! How did the audit go?"

"It's still going. Kate overheard one of them say three days wasn't nearly enough, not when they were having such a field day."

"Well, that's great, isn't it? That they're enjoying themselves, I mean. It must be going really well."

She sighed. "Just try and keep out of their way, Morten. Don't tell them anything, don't engage in conversation and don't make eye contact. If they ask you something, just refer them straight to me. Have you got that?"

"Yes, no problem." I beamed at Joy and glanced around to make sure we couldn't be overheard. "Can you keep a secret, Joy? I've got something to tell you."

"Will it affect your work in anyway?"

"Er, no, I don't think so-"

"Then I don't need to know, do I? Get your headset on, keep your head down and don't look up again until I tell you to."

Monday mornings were always extremely busy, so it was difficult to perform a proper search of baby websites, but I found one entitled 'An expectant Dad's guide to pregnancy' and kept it minimised, flicking back to it whenever a customer launched into a lengthy rant or a prolonged spell of weeping. The first line read: 'The thing about men and pregnancy is that there's only so much you can do - the expectant mother really does all the work'. Blimey, it was going to be easier than I thought! Mum often joked that Dad only took an interest in me when I became old enough to go and buy his fags from the off licence. Little did she know I started doing this when I was six! Dad always made sure I put on a reflective armband if it was dark when he sent me out;

Helper' written on it. "It's just a bit of fun! She'll love it, won't she?"

Mum frowned. "But the baby won't be born until July, Morto. It'll look a bit silly wearing a Christmas outfit in the middle of summer."

"Oh." I hadn't thought of that. "I'll have to send it back. If I can. What do you think I should get Myra?"

"Now, don't go spending too much, son - remember you've got to give me a bit extra for the house-keeping over the next few weeks to cover the cost of Christmas lunch. It's really expensive entertaining, you know."

"I thought you were getting everything free from the food bank? Didn't that nice man say he could get you a massive turkey if you gave him one of your lessons?"

"I've already given him one! And it turned out he didn't work there at all - no one actually knew who he was!" Mum sniffed. "Anyway, we did have that lovely chocolate cake last week, didn't we? I told them it was your tenth birthday and you weren't getting any presents, so they got it in for me specially."

"Wow, free chocolate cake – this country is really amazing."

There was another rehearsal at the Jubilee Hall tonight and this time, I was involved! I had to award a diploma to the Scarecrow, a clockwork heart to the Tin Man and I tried to pin a medal onto the Lion, but Frankie put me off by growling in my face, "I bet you're enjoying fondling my tits, aren't you, bender?" which made my fingers all fumbly.

Tom the Director yelled, "The bloody audience will be covered in cobwebs by the time you've finished!" I then had to practise stepping into a large cardboard box with Myra, pretending it was a hot air balloon, but our heads clashed as we bent down to get in and she snapped, "For fucks sake, you clumsy sodding oaf!"

"Myra!" I gasped, shocked. "The baby can hear everything you say, you know! I've been reading up about it; you mustn't swear in front of it - you'll stunt its vocabulary."

There was a stunned silence. "Nice one Foggy," Myra muttered.

"What was that?" asked Tom.

"Ignore Foggy," Myra told him, shooting me a ferocious look. "He's the one that's stunted - in the head."

"What was that about a baby?" Tom persisted.

"Myra and I are expecting a baby," I said proudly, putting my arm as far around Myra as I could and giving her a big squeeze. She shrugged me off and glared defiantly at Tom, who'd gone white. "Don't worry, Tom!" I laughed. "The baby's not due for ages. Myra didn't want anyone to know yet, but I seem to have let the cat out of the bag! Well, no one need be concerned - Myra's condition won't affect her wonderful performance as Dorothy. In fact, all those extra hormones will probably enhance it."

Tom didn't seem to know what to say and the rest of the cast were staring at us, too surprised to offer congratulations. Thin Lizzie eventually broke the silence.

"Well I never, Dorothy's up the duff! Don't remember that from the film. Still, we could use it to our advantage, couldn't we, Tom? Bring this production bang up to date, so to speak - perhaps we could say the Cowardly Lion got Dorothy pregnant - that would take a real show of courage, wouldn't it? To shag *that*, I mean."

Myra shrieked and launched herself at Thin Lizzie. I tried to grab hold of her arm, but she brushed me off, sending me sprawling across the cardboard box, completely flattening it. "Stop them Tom!" I cried, as the two girls started fighting again, but Tom had sunk onto his haunches at the edge of stage, looking somewhat shattered. I struggled to my feet and edged hesitantly towards the girls, taking care to dodge the blows.

Luckily, I was on the late shift today, so I had time to pop into Superdrug before work to get some Savlon to put on the scratches. Only the very deepest ones were still bleeding. When I got into the office and approached my desk, I saw, to my astonishment, that there was the outline of a figure marked in chalk on the carpet, right by my chair. Oh my God! Had someone been killed in the office? Why had they died at my desk? Surely they couldn't have tripped over my ergonomic tilting footrest, could they – I kept it next to my chair so I could sit sideways and read Derek's Auto Trader during calls - but what if they had, what if they'd fallen over it and banged their head? I'd murdered someone, or manslaughtered them, at the very least. I could go to prison, I'd never see my child, and they'd grow up to think their father was a notorious jailbird, like Peter Sutcliff or Jeffrey Archer. *Oh God.*

"What happened?" I mouthed across the desk to Sky, who was on a call. She shrugged at me. "Look, all I'm trying to do is help you, Mr Caple. Oh, right, Mrs Caple. There's no need to be so aggressive. I'm sorry you're having to live in a caravan in your back garden, but why don't you look at it as a kind of holiday? You know, find the positives-"

I went over to Gay Ray and tapped him urgently on the shoulder. He was reading an article on premature ejaculation. "Ray, what on earth's happened? Who died at my desk?"

"You'd better ask Tim," he said, without looking up. "I've got issues of my own to deal with." I turned to face Tim, who was grinning very broadly in my direction. How could he possibly think this was funny? Why was he smiling like that? Unless ... oh, of course - it was a joke! No one had actually died, it was just another of the team's little pranks. *Thank goodness.* Weak with relief, I sank into my chair and switched my workstation on with trembling hands. I should have been better prepared; those on the late shift often arrived to some jolly jape or other - Alan still hadn't noticed the word "Prick" written in Tippex on the bottom of his black mug. You'd think he'd wonder why everyone sniggered each time he drained his tea.

My heart rate returning to normal, I began to untangle my headset and made sure the footrest was tucked right away under my desk. Sky ended her call with "People in the third world would kill to live in a caravan, you know!" She jabbed the call release button on her turret and sighed. "I can't stand all this negative karma today, it's going to bring my hives up again. You've heard what's going on, haven't you?"

"No, what?"

She leant forward over the blue soundboard. "Someone's only gone and shot their mouth off to the auditors. Told them we weren't following procedures, didn't record complaints properly and that there's password sharing going on..." Sky broke off as she glanced over her shoulder to see if she could be overheard. "Joy and Kate are in a crisis meeting with their boss at the moment; he's come down specially."

I whistled. The Ginger Slug Balancer, as Tim called him, only made an occasional appearance, so things must be very bad indeed. "Who do you think it was, Sky?" I asked. "Who would say those sorts of things?"

"Hmmm, I'm not sure, but I take my bloody hat off to them - blowing the whistle on the fascist movement! I'd like to shake them by the hand."

Everything fell silent as an ashen-faced Joy scurried into the department, rummaged around in her drawers for her inhaler and then hurried off again. Tim came over, still grinning. "You're back from the dead then, Fogster? Or are you an apparition?" He peered at me. "Blimey! Kate's had her claws into you already, I see; I had a feeling she might tear you limb from limb."

"Oh no, that was Myra," I said, touching my face gingerly. Tim didn't seem to know what to say to that. Sky nodded sympathetically as she shuffled her pack of tarot cards. "I warned you about those hormones, didn't I? Shall I do you a reading, Foggy, see what's in store for your future?"

Tim snorted. "How many times can you turn up the grim reaper?"

Sky ignored him and spread the cards face down over her desk, closing her eyes as she waved her hands over the cards, 'transferring her energy'. This was exciting! I held my breath as she slowly turned one of the cards over. The Fool. Tim snorted again. Sky frowned and concentrated hard on the cards. Her hands stopped at another and she was just about to turn it over when a loud shout made us all jump.

"THERE'S FORTY CALLS QUEUING! ANSWER THE SODDING THINGS!"

Kate was standing in the department, eyes bulging. Tim shot back to his desk and everyone else stopped texting or put down their magazines and whipped their headsets on. Gay Ray had a look of horror frozen onto his face; I saw Sky pass him a box of tissues. I took a call from a Mrs Chumbly about her flooding and when Kate finally stalked off, I leant over the soundboard and picked up the card that Sky had been about to reveal. It was The Fool again. I sighed. Perhaps Myra was right about this sort of thing, maybe it is all a load of mumbo-jumbo. I turned my attention back to Mrs Chumbly, concerned to hear that her damp patch was spreading.

I was feeling very perky when I arrived for my Sunday shift at Smokey Joe's. Having just been paid by Perypils, I'd managed to get some Christmas shopping done on Saturday, although once I'd given Mum the additional house-keeping, I was already overdrawn. But not to worry - Joe owed me for the last six Sundays, so that should put me back in the black. Poor Myra couldn't come shopping as her mum told me she was being sick when I called round. Her mum said, "That will teach her to drink eight pints of snakebite." How funny! As if Myra would touch alcohol while she's pregnant. Her mum was such a card, she was going to be a brilliant Granny.

I gave her some information to pass onto Myra that I'd printed from the Internet. It showed foetal development at ten weeks. "Look what it says about the reflexes!" I exclaimed excitedly. "It says he can curl his toes and clench his fingers!"

"Yep, I bet he's shaking his fists right now."

"He looks just like a peanut, doesn't he?"

"That's all we need; another nut-job in the family."

I hadn't been able to stop myself from buying another baby gift for Peanut when I saw an animal alphabet wall canvas, which was reduced to £4.99 in BHS. Some of the animals were a bit random - I wasn't sure myself what an ibex was and the yeti was the stuff of nightmares - but at least it would introduce Peanut to his letters. I wanted him to grow up to be really brainy, to study hard and have a great career. Maybe he'd even follow in my footsteps and land a fantastic job in a call centre - what a brilliant future he would have! I caught myself; *he* might well be a *she*. I knew I shouldn't care, but I had to admit I would love to have a son so I could replicate the close bond I had with my father. I'd do all the things with Peanut that Dad had wanted to do with me if only his work hadn't got in the way: fishing in the canal, football in the park, camping in the back garden - hopefully, when Dad found out he was going to be a grandfather, he would move back to Shodsworth and join in with all the family fun he'd missed out on before. I'd send Dad another letter tonight, the last one must have gone astray. I heard Mum saying to the Inland Revenue that it was a very busy time of year for the post office, and that was probably why they hadn't received her cheque yet.

It took me a while to realise what was missing when I flicked the lights on in the cafe. Where was the coffee machine? I stared at the huge gap on the counter, which was only partly filled by a yellow Kenwood kettle and a tin of Tesco's Everyday Value coffee. I hunted all round the cafe to see if Joe was hiding from me again, but there was no sign of him. Gosh, this was tricky. It was the second Sunday of the month and the Shodsworth Scientology group would be in for their cappuccinos; some of them were extremely particular about the thickness of their froth and would accuse me of 'limiting their material happiness' if I didn't get it exactly right. I found a whisk in the kitchen and washed something brown and sticky from it. It should be ok, as long as I whipped vigorously enough.

As I opened up, Freckly Girl appeared in the doorway. "Oh, hello!" I said. "You're early today."

She laughed. "I couldn't sleep! How are you? How's rehearsals?"

"Good thanks, but it's the final run-through this week and I'm really nervous. I don't feel nearly prepared enough."

"I'm sure you'll be brilliant. Can I book a ticket in advance?"

"Oh, just turn up on the night, there's plenty of space in the hall. Bring a chair though, so you don't have to sit on a broken one."

I flicked the kettle on. "Where's the coffee machine?" she asked in surprise.

"Um, I'm not sure. I think Joe might have taken it to be serviced, or something..."

"So, Joe's not here either? But how are you going to-"

Three workmen bundled into the cafe and sat down with a noisy scraping of chairs, and, I think, a fart. "Three breakfasts and three coffees, mate," one of them called, opening his Nuts magazine. "Fast as you like."

"I've never cooked a full breakfast before," I whispered to Freckly Girl. "It's not difficult, is it?"

"I'll do it," she said, removing her coat. "You get their coffees."

"No, I can't ask you to-" I tried to protest, but she was already on her way to the kitchen. Could she cook? Shouldn't she have a certificate or something before she served the public? Tim told me that all red-haired people suffered from something called gingervitus - was it transferable to the food chain? I waited for the kettle to boil as bacon smells started to waft through from the kitchen, causing the workmen to keep looking round impatiently. Freckly Girl eventually appeared with the breakfasts. "There you are guys!" she said brightly. "Sorry about the wait; I've given you all a free hash brown by way of apology!" They seemed perfectly happy with that and set upon the food like they hadn't eaten in months.

"Thank you so much," I said to her. "Where did you learn to cook so well?"

"I used to help out in the kitchens at Shodsworth Manor, you know, the old people's home. Voluntary, of course. It's closed down now - Government cuts, you understand, not food poisoning!"

I laughed. Behind her, the door flew open and Barry lurched in. "Watcha Fog. Do us a bacon sarnie, will you? I'm hanging out of my arse."

Freckly Girl smiled and returned to the kitchen. Barry peered after her. "Who's that? Has Joe lost a lot of weight or am I still pissed from last night?"

"Oi, mate," one of the workmen called to me. "This coffee's shite."

"Don't pick on the coffee," Barry reprimanded. "It's too weak to fight back."

"I'll make some more," I said, putting the kettle on again. "I opened up this morning to find the coffee machine had vanished."

"Oh yeah? Along with Joe, by any chance? I wondered how long before he scarpered."

I stared at him. "What do you mean?"

"Up to his neck in debts, isn't he?" He took his sandwich from Freckly Girl. "And let's face it, he was hardly going to win a Michelin star for this shit, was he?"

"But - he trained with Gordon Ramsay!"

Barry choked on the first mouthful. "Yeah, that's true, he did! I saw it on the telly - Gordon Behind Bars it was called. Set in Brixton prison."

"Oh no, they were at Claridges together-"

"Ha ha!" Barry roared with laughter and jabbed me in the ribs. "Good one, Foggy! Anyway, how's the beast? I see she hasn't had her talons clipped lately - look at the state of your face! You can't fight nature, I suppose - first the claws, then the horns, then the pointy tail."

I leant forward conspiratorially and lowered my voice. "Myra's pregnant, Barry."

His mouth fell open. A piece of half-chewed crust dropped out. "W-w-well, it's nothing to do with me! Why, what's she said?"

"Of course it's nothing to do with you! It's not your fault I used sub-standard condoms, is it? Sorry," I said to the shocked Scientologists, who'd chosen that moment to come in. "I've got to take responsibility for my actions. I can't wait to be a dad, actually. I know I shouldn't say it, but I can't help hoping for a boy. We can do all that father and son stuff, you know? I'd love it to be a boy, I really would."

Barry chewed his sandwich thoughtfully. "I think The Omen's on Channel 4 again tonight."

Dress Rehearsal

I arrived at work a little earlier so I could ask Kate if there was any overtime going. Joe hadn't come into the cafe at all on Sunday, so Freckly Girl had stayed all day to help out, although we hadn't been very busy. Joe owed me for six Sundays and I needed the money so I could finish my Christmas shopping. I'd tried calling him, but there was no reply. Oh well, nothing for it, I'd just have to use more of my overdraft, although Tim suggested I tried a Payday loan, because they had a fantastic reputation and hardly charged you any interest. That sounded ideal. I resolved to Google them between calls.

It was difficult to hear my customers over Sky's noisy sobbing. She returned from a meeting with Kate wailing, "They think it's me! The bastards think I'm the supergrass!" We tried to comfort her with soothing cups of herbal tea and rabbit chanting, but she was extremely distressed, even clutching my arm and crying, "Don't let this happen to me, Foggy, don't let me get dicked by the corporate knobs!" I didn't know what to say to her and I felt completely torn in two, as in my headset, my customer was also sobbing: "You can't do this to me, you can't! How can you say it wasn't a storm - my roof has a massive great hole in it, you can see right into the kids' bedroom, for Christ's sake! You've got to pay out!"

It was a pretty stressful morning all in all, but I did manage to grab a quick word with Kate as she passed through the department, carrying a huge coffee and a packet of Calms. "Hi Kate! Did you get up to anything nice at the weekend?"

"I visited some burial sites. To choose a plot."

"Oh, how lovely. Did you select one?"

"I did select one, yes. But it's not for me."

"Er, right. Is there any chance of overtime, Kate? I could really use some extra cash you see, so I can finish my shopping-"

"You've only just been paid, Morten."

"Yes, I know, but I had to give my Mum extra this month and well, you see, I'd like to get Myra something really special, as she's expecting."

"What's she expecting?"

"Oh, I wasn't supposed to say!" I laughed out loud - I'd done it again! "We're going to have a baby."

Kate stared at me. "*You're* going to reproduce?"

"Yes," I said proudly. "There's going to be another little Foggy introduced to the world - imagine that!"

Kate looked down at her packet of Calms and muttered something I couldn't quite hear, although I thought I caught the word 'cyanide'. She walked off, still muttering. I assumed that meant there wasn't going to be any overtime. Never mind - I'd just have to give the nice Payday loans people a call.

It was time for my very first dress rehearsal in the lead role. I don't think I'd ever been so exhilarated cycling to the Jubilee Hall. With the Boxing Day opening night just a week away, excitement was beginning to build, and with everyone in their fabulous costumes, it really felt as if the performance had sprung to life.

Barry had actually turned up and was relishing his costume, lifting his dress to flash the girls, causing shrieks of horror. I hoped he would have a shave before opening night

and that Tom would make him cover up his tattoo of a naked
Betty Boop bending over - it didn't seem like the sort of thing
Auntie Em would have. Frankie Trevino kept throwing his
flick knife at Nervous Noel to see if he could make it stick
into his Tin Man outfit (a dustbin with the bottom burnt out)
and Thin Lizzie was trying to coax Toto out of his basket
with a digestive biscuit. Tom the Director was having trouble
with a new PA system that he'd installed; he couldn't get it to
work properly so every now and then the hall was filled with
" for f......... why don't you... what a f .... piece of sh....."

As we were waiting to get started, I managed to grab a
quick word with Myra as she adjusted the straps on her pretty
gingham pinafore. "Myra, I got this leaflet for you, one of my
customers gave it to me. There's a really interesting section
on childbirth."

"Oh yeah?"

"It's all about giving birth silently, I'll read you a bit. It
says: any words spoken are recorded in the reactive mind and
can have a harmful effect on the child. So, ideally, the doctors
and nurses shouldn't speak to you and you must try not to
make a sound-"

"Are you taking the complete piss?"

"Er, I think it sounds-"

"Have you ever tried shitting a bowling ball?"

"Um, well, no-"

"Then shut up."

I realised I hadn't chosen a very sensible time to broach
the subject, so I carefully folded the leaflet in two and tucked
it into the pocket of my jeans. I didn't have a costume to
wear as Tom said the Wizard is "just a regular guy". I had
come across an old Santa Claus outfit in the props cupboard,

so I was wearing the long white curly wig to make myself look a bit more wizardy. The beard was missing so I'd made one out of a roll of cotton wool I'd found in the first aid box at work. Just think - next year I'd have a child to share Christmas with! I could take Peanut to visit Father Christmas in that magical grotto outside Dorothy Perkins. Granny Pattern had taken me there once, but it was spoilt when she got very upset about the present I'd been given; a pink plastic teacup and saucer, for a doll's house. Personally, I think the £3 fee was more about the experience and I'm not sure it warranted Gran's two-hour sit-down protest on top of the elf.

Tom's voice boomed over the PA. "Right, you shower of sh.... let's get this ... ...on the road. And if I see anyone ....king yawning this time, I'm going to shove this ...... right up your .... First positions, everyone."

How very exciting - we were off!

I wheeled my bicycle slowly home. Its tyres had been completely slashed, even though I'd tucked it away behind the wheelie bins in the car park. Bloomin' kids. I hoped Peanut didn't grow up to be a horrid vandal. The dress rehearsal had gone quite well, apart from the fire, but at least we had managed to get it under control before it reached the helium canisters. I don't know why Frankie chose to fiddle with his lighter when he was standing right next to the Scarecrow, but luckily the bucket of water destined for the Wicked Witch managed to put out most of the Scarecrow's clothes. Shame he'd already run round the stage in a panic and set the curtains alight, but they'd burnt themselves out just before Tom managed to get the fire extinguisher to work.

Before the fire, poor Myra had experienced a few technical difficulties with her performance; her breasts had bounced out of her pinafore dress during the 'Yellow Brick Road' - Nervous Noel had to sit down and breathe into a paper bag until his panic attack subsided. When Glinda the Good Witch tried to transfer the ruby slippers to Myra's feet, it took two of the cast the best part of twenty minutes to unlace Myra's Doc Martens, tug them off her and wrestle her feet into the slippers. All the Munchkins started kicking off, moaning "Can't we stand up for a bit, our knees are bloody killing us" and when Frankie changed some lyrics to "Lions and Tigers and Big Foot, oh my!", Myra attacked him with the Tin Man's axe. Thankfully, it was just a pretend one, made from rubber; the real one had gone missing. Tom had offered to drive Myra home, which was very kind of him, I think my slashed tyres may have proved too much for her to bear. I pondered the evening's events as I walked home. I couldn't help feeling a little disappointed with my contribution, especially as the starring character. I didn't even get to use my powerful wizard's voice that I'd perfected. Tom got Trunky Tracy to do it over the PA system as he said her voice was "more imposing" than mine. I did get to hand out the awards at the end and then wave goodbye to everyone from a cardboard box as two of the cast covered me over with paper clouds.

I was still deep in thought as I turned into the drive, and wheeled my flaccid tyres right over a smashed Smirnoff bottle. It was a piece of luck they were already in tatters. I found Mum in the lounge watching Crimewatch, so I made us a cup of tea and sat through a scary reconstruction of a bank robbery. One of the men caught on CCTV looked just like Joe. How funny, Chef has a double! I couldn't wait to tell him.

It was Christmas Eve at last, the second most wonderful day of the year. It was bitterly cold and I struggled to cycle with any speed into a freezing north-easterly wind. "Morning Joy," I mumbled through numb lips when I reached the office. I tried to turn my computer on, but my fingers just wouldn't work.

"Hurry up, Morten," Joy snapped, impatiently. "You're late and we're short on bodies today, so get yourself logged in and pick up some of these calls."

"Is someone off sick?" I asked Tim, who was playing online golf and eating a mince pie.

"I should imagine Sky's feeling pretty sick," he replied. "She's been suspended."

"*What?*" I gasped, shocked beyond belief. "Why?"

"They believe she's the whistle-blower! Jackie sits next to the meeting room and heard the whole thing. Kate accused Sky of bringing the company into disrepute and breaching security procedures. Sky strongly denied it of course, but Kate was having none of it and marched her out the door."

"I can't believe it." My first call of the day bleeped in my ear, as my turret told me they had been waiting for twenty-three minutes, but my stiff fingers missed the 'Answer' button and hit 'Release' instead. Oh dear. Hopefully they'd call back again. "Surely there must be some mistake; Sky wouldn't say awful things about the company - I can't imagine who would."

"Can't you?" asked Tim. "Can't you really?"

"No! How dreadful for her, and on Christmas Eve! But what about all her stuff, you know, her crystals and cards-"

"Chuck 'em, they're obviously faulty - I mean, she didn't see that one coming, did she?"

I felt terrible for Sky and although Tim said we weren't allowed to contact her, I popped one of the leaflets the Scientologists had given me into the post for her. I thought she might find it comforting to know that 'difficulties with nagging insecurities, self-doubt and despair can be overcome as man innately possesses the potential to be free of these'. I added the letters 'wo' in front of 'man' with my biro as I thought Sky would appreciate that; she once told me she didn't shave her armpits as a protest against men's oppression. I planned to talk to Myra over Christmas about giving birth silently, when she was in a more relaxed mood. I'd asked Barry if he thought it was a good idea to do it silently, without all the agonised wailing and screaming, but he'd assumed I was talking about the conception.

Although I was shocked and upset for Sky, I couldn't help feeling excited about Christmas. I updated Facebook and Twitter with seasons greetings while I waited for a man with a stutter to explain his complaint to me; he took so long I managed to write all my Christmas cards as well.

The food bank parcel had arrived last night, delivered by a very nice man who stayed and had a glass of wine with Mum. He must have forgotten something because I saw him walking out of our gate this morning when I drew my curtains. How kind of him to come all the way back on Christmas morning! Such wonderful dedication to duty.

Downstairs, the turkey was almost defrosted, so I helped Mum run it under the hot tap while the oven was getting up to temperature. "Do you think it's big enough for all of us, Mum?" I asked, doubtfully.

"We'll just have to fill up the plates with chipolatas," said Mum. "There's bloody hundreds of those."

"Well, you did tell the food bank man that you were partial to a nice hot sausage," I laughed. "So he must have slipped you an extra large portion!"

"That's debatable."

"Shall I start peeling the potatoes? Gosh, they're bright green! Are they supposed to be that colour?"

"He said they came from Greenland. It's next to Iceland, apparently."

"A new name on the high street! And they say we're in a recession!" I picked up the peeler. "What do you think Dad's doing today?"

Mum scrolled through her Christmas playlist and selected 'Fairy Tale of New York'. She said it always reminded her of Dad. "I don't really know what he'll be doing, son. Slopping out, I expect."

"You mean slobbing out, Mum! He always likes to relax on Christmas Day, doesn't he? Do you remember that year he spent the entire day asleep on the sofa? We even pulled crackers and party poppers all round him and he didn't stir!"

"Yes, I remember." Mum was thrusting her hand inside the turkey rather violently and I looked at her in alarm; she always got a little stressed preparing Christmas lunch for everyone, and I hoped we wouldn't have a repeat of last year when she'd smashed her fist into the Christmas pudding just because Myra asked her what time we would be eating. We were still coming across bits of candied peel stuck around the kitchen.

The doorbell rang and Mum groaned. "Oh God, that will be your Gran. Bloody lunchtime, I told her - it's only half past nine! Get your garlic and crucifix, son and let her in. And hide the brandy in your room, would you - she's sussed out the cistern safe-place. Nose like a bloodhound."

The kitchen was filled with happy chatter and lovely roast dinner smells. Auntie Trisha was filling everyone's glasses with more sparkling wine, except for her wife's: Biffa only drank Guinness. The food bank mince pies had been opened - well, they'd arrived that way - but I couldn't eat another thing. Myra had her foot up on the table showing off her new scull toe-ring that her mother had given her and I was showing Biffa what the foetus would look like from the app on my iPhone. "Do you want to look too, Gran?" I asked. "See - your great-grandchild looks just like a peanut at the moment!"

Granny Pattern sniffed. "It looks like a bastard peanut to me." She pointed a bony finger at Myra. "It would never have been tolerated in my day, never! The shame would have been enough to kill a person, but now these brazen hussies just flaunt it in your face everywhere you go. I have to fight a path through semi-naked teenagers and pushchairs just to get into Lidls."

"Things are a bit different now Mum, thank Christ!" laughed Auntie Trisha, planting a kiss on the top of Biffa's new crew cut. "I mean, just look at us!"

Granny Pattern clutched at her throat. "What would my Arthur say?" she wailed. "His family, torn apart by infidelity and riddled with debauchery, his only grandchild-" she fixed me with her beady eyes "led astray by a wanton strumpet, his chastity corrupted-"

"Have I strayed into Iran?" asked Mum, who'd been having a cigarette in the garden. "What's that ghastly thing on your toe, Myra? You shouldn't be wasting your money on that sort of rubbish, not with a baby on the way. Raising children is extremely expensive, you know."

Myra bristled. "Yes it is, Pam, and as Foggy will want to provide for his child, he won't be able to give you as much house-keeping as he does now."

"Why, you little-" Mum caught herself. "You'll get a small fortune in benefits-"

"Like you get a small fortune in house-keeping? It's outrageous the amount he has to give you-"

"Woah - time out!" called Auntie Trisha, making a T sign with her hands. "No arguing at Christmas, that's the rule! Come on, let's open the presents."

Yay - presents! The best part of the whole day. We all went into the lounge, apart from Granny Pattern who said she was going to the toilet to "give things a go"; she thought that Mum's giblet pâté might have loosened her up a bit. I loved opening presents but not as much as I loved watching others open theirs. I received a Sainsbury's giftcard from Mum (she didn't have time to get to Halfords) and a Brut soap-on-the-rope from Gran. Myra got me a mini carpet golf set, in case I ever took up golf, which was really thoughtful of her, and there was a present from Dad under the tree! He always sent me something. I opened up the brown packet, my fingers trembling with excitement. I unwrapped a large wooden fork and then a rather wonky wooden spoon. I held them up, mystified.

"Salad servers," explained Auntie Trisha. "By the look of them, I'd say they were home-made."

Wow! Dad had actually made me a present, how wonderful. I turned them over and over in my hands, marvelling at his craftsmanship. Dad really could turn his hand to anything! "What have you got for Myra?" Mum asked me. I smiled conspiratorially at Myra.

"I chose some very special presents for Myra, as this has been such an amazing year." I picked up her presents and placed them in her lap. She looked a little disappointed.

"None of these look big enough to be the leather bondage platform boots I asked for, Foggy." She started to unwrap one with a sigh, and then squealed with delight as she recognised the Chucky DVD box set. "Stick one of these on, Pam!" she cried. "Anything's better than that old bat droning on about the Commonwealth." She unwrapped the next present to reveal a tiny, white babygro. "Oh, er, right. Thanks."

"Turn it over Myra!" I urged. She held it up to reveal 'FOGGY JUNIOR' printed on the back. Everyone went "Awww" and Myra seemed completely overcome; she was unable to speak. She slowly unwrapped her third present, clearly savouring the moment, and found a pink china mug. It had 'World's Best Mum' written on it. She stared at it for a moment and then burst into tears. "Hormones," everyone said in unison. Granny Pattern reappeared.

"No luck, Pam," she announced. "Pass us those salad servers and I'll give it another go."

Boxing Night

Everyone had gone to The White Horse, as was the tradition on Boxing Day, but I decided to stay home to make sure I was fresh for tonight's performance. I wrote a letter to Dad telling him all about our wonderful Christmas and thanking him for my lovely salad servers. I asked if he could make me another fork as unfortunately the original had split in two. I reminded Dad that this time next year I would be a father myself, and Peanut would be five months old already - a proper little person! And tonight, I would be making my debut in a starring role. I must make sure someone records it so I can show it to Peanut when he's old enough. It might inspire him to tread the boards too, just like Gareth Gates had inspired me when he took over the role of Joseph, just before the show ended.

The Jubilee Hall was a blaze of lights and a buzz of excited voices; opening night was terrifying yet exhilarating at the same time. Myra was on stage practising her breathing exercises as Tom watched over her, the Scarecrow was shedding straw all over the place and Frankie Trevino was loosening the screws on the Tin Man's dustbin with a spanner, because Nervous Noel was beginning to feel claustrophobic. I found Barry backstage sprawled across a chair in his Auntie Em dress. His eyes were shut but he opened one as I sat down next to him; it was extremely bloodshot and there was a deep gash across his forehead. "Just woke up under a Ford Focus," he grunted. "No idea how I got there."

"Oh dear! Are you going to be alright for your performance, Bazza?" I asked anxiously.

"Who gives a shit? Just got to wail 'Daisy, oh Daisy', a few times, haven't I? Shouldn't be difficult."

"It's Dorothy."

"Whatever."

The audience was beginning to arrive at the hall, so I went out front to show people to their seats, although they could sit anywhere they liked, of course. Mum came with Auntie Trisha and Biffa, so I made sure they had chairs in the front row, and Gay Ray from work turned up too. He told Mum he adored Judy Garland. I felt a hand on my arm as I was moving a broken chair to one side and turned to see Freckly Girl at my elbow. "Oh, hello!" I said. "How nice of you to come."

"I wasn't sure if it would be going ahead, I read about the fire in the paper. I would have phoned you, but I haven't got your contact details."

"It was only a small fire, hardly worthy of mention in the grand Shodsworth News!"

"Shall we exchange phone numbers anyway, I mean, in case we do need to contact each other?"

"Oh, don't worry," I laughed. "There's unlikely to be another disaster anytime soon! Lightening doesn't strike twice, you know!" I jumped as a piercing scream rang out from the stage and I saw Thin Lizzie frozen in terror with the end of her broomstick in flames. Quick-thinking Tom grabbed it from her and beat it out against the dustbin. Nervous Noel did extremely well to keep his footing. "For Christ's sake Frankie!" Tom yelled. "How many times do I have to tell you; stop lighting your bloody cigarettes in here!

And somebody chuck that bucket of water over the haystack - there's smoke coming from it!"

Freckly Girl seemed about to say something to me but she was interrupted by the arrival of Granny Pattern.

"Got any cushions, Morten? I need to sit on something that will deaden the sound. Blame your mother's Brussel sprouts; like rubber bullets, they were, I reckon they'll stay lodged in my colon 'til New Year."

As I selected some dry straw from the haystack for Granny Pattern to sit on, I felt my heart beginning to race. Not long now and the curtain would be coming up on my first performance as the lead actor; I'd better go and get my cotton wool beard on!

The after show party was always tremendous fun, and I munched on a selection of party nibbles with Mum, Auntie Trisha and Biffa as we reflected on another triumphant evening for the SADS. "Myra was simply awesome, wasn't she?" I said, proudly, biting into a mini picnic egg.

"That's one word for it," said Mum, rubbing her forehead. "Didn't really need that microphone though, did she? It's a miracle only one speaker blew."

"A pity the PA system is a bit dodgy," added Auntie Trisha. "Poor Myra thought it had cut out during Somewhere Over the Rainbow, didn't she? Unless the lyric actually was 'someday I'll wish upon a star and beat the living shit out of you, you utter fucking piece of crap'."

"Oh, I thought she'd got away with that," I said, dismayed. "And it cut out during the Tin Man's song as well."

"That didn't matter," said Biffa, supportively. "He was shaking so hard you couldn't hear anything over the sound of his dustbin rattling."

"I did feel sorry for him," said Mum. "Especially when Barry was sick into the dustbin; Noel did very well to carry on, I think."

Granny Pattern joined us, trying to get her handbag to close over two dozen sausage rolls. "Did you enjoy my performance, Gran?" I asked.

"Were you in it?"

"Yes! I handed out the awards at the end and took off in the balloon."

"Why didn't you wake me, Pam?" she asked my mother crossly.

"I thought you'd passed away," my mother muttered, under her breath. "Wishful bloody thinking."

"Why were you dressed as Santa Claus?" Auntie Trisha asked me.

"I thought you were Colonel Sanders!" exclaimed Biffa. "I kept thinking I could murder a KFC."

"Where's Myra?" asked Mum. "Not still upset about Toto, is she? She was a bit heavy-handed with the poor little thing. I'm not surprised he went for her. Dogs don't like being grabbed by their balls, you know. Or chucked into haystacks."

"I don't know why they didn't use a bitch for Toto," mumbled Granny Pattern. "They used one for Dorothy."

"I think Myra was more shaken by the Wicked Witch not dying when she was supposed to," I told them. "Everyone was taken by surprise when the witch came back to life and attempted to garrotte Dorothy with the broomstick. I'm sure that wasn't in rehearsals."

"Perhaps you'd better go and find Myra," said Mum. "Check she's ok."

"I'll see if she's in the toilets," said Granny Pattern, "I'm heading that way. Now, don't you go home without me, Pam; I don't want to get locked in there overnight again."

I was just about to go outside to look for Myra when the PA system crackled into life and her voice filled the hall.

"I've told you, Tom - I don't know!"

"You do know, Myra! It's mine, isn't it?"

"Foggy thinks it's-" the system broke up on Myra's reply.

"That stupid lit........ker! When are you going to tell the poor .... truth?"

"You want ..... get rid ..... don't you? In case your idiot wife ...."

"You leave my wife ....   she's not ...." There was a pause. "Don't tell me that bloody thing's on? What the ......"

The hall had fallen silent. I looked around and everyone seemed to be staring at me. What was wrong? The curtain hiding the PA system was pulled back very slowly and Tom and Myra appeared hesitantly from behind it. "There you are Myra!" I exclaimed. "We wondered where you'd got to. Come and try these pigs in blankets."

"Myra's had quite enough pigs in blankets by the sound of it," Mum said, very loudly. "I think she's got some explaining to do."

Myra fiddled with her plaits and looked sideways at Tom. "Um, shall we go outside, do you think, and-"

"No, I don't think we will." Mum sounded angry, for some reason. "I think you'll stand right there on that stage in front of everyone and tell us the truth. Loud and clear please, Myra, so we can all hear you. Whose baby are you expecting?"

I stared at Mum. Had she gone mad? Perhaps she'd had too much to drink, she had been knocking back the Lambrini at an alarming rate. Myra's eyes darted wildly round the hall and settled on Tom, but he was looking down at his shoes.

"Is it Tom's baby?" Mum demanded.

"Mum!" I hissed. "I warned you about watching too much Jeremy Kyle! Of course it's not Tom's baby; Peanut's one hundred percent pure Fogarty!" I beamed up at Myra. "Tell her, Myra." She looked down at me miserably and didn't speak. It was so quiet in the hall I could hear my heart thudding in my ears. "Myra?" I choked, my throat suddenly dry.

"I'm sorry, Foggy."

There was silence for a moment, then Mum let out a strangled yelp and launched herself towards the stage. Biffa, who used to be a bouncer, made a grab for her and hung on for dear life as Mum wriggled and kicked, screaming dreadful obscenities up at Myra. Biffa managed to drag her outside, shouting, "Leave it Pam, leave it!"

"W-what are you saying, Myra?" I stammered. "You don't mean ... you can't mean, you're not saying that, that Peanut isn't mine?"

"I'm sorry, Foggy," she said again, big tears rolling down her cheeks. "He's not yours."

"He's mine," said Tom, lifting his head to look at me. "I'm the father."

"Er, well, actually you might not be," mumbled Myra, wiping her nose with her hand.

"*What?*"

Myra gazed down at her ruby slippers. "It could be Frankie's-"

There was a loud crash as the Cowardly Lion dropped his bottle of Becks. A cigarette fell from his open mouth.

"Or, it might be someone else's..." Myra raised her head and several of the Munchkins examined their fingernails. Barry vomited into the cardboard box hot air balloon.

"Jesus Christ!" burst out Auntie Trisha. "There's a cast of bloody thousands! Shame on you, Myra - how *could you* let Foggy think he was the father? You're sick in the head!"

I didn't hear the rest of the ferocious row that broke out in the hall. I was vaguely aware of Tom shouting, Frankie swearing, Myra sobbing, Barry heaving, Thin Lizzie laughing.... but I could only lean against a trestle table in a daze. Peanut wasn't mine. I wasn't going to be his Dad. There wouldn't be father and son fishing expeditions, or camping in the garden, or trips to Millets to select the best lightweight waterproof cycling trousers. None of that was going to happen now.

I had the sensation of everything falling away. Someone was talking to me and my eyes slowly focussed on Freckly Girl, who was peering at me anxiously. "Do you want to go home, Morten? I can walk with you, if you'd like."

"I've got my bike," I said, distractedly. There was a loud crash as Tom overturned a table to get to Frankie and chairs started to fly across the hall. "I think, perhaps, I will go home."

Freckly Girl followed me out and we passed Granny Pattern who was coming from the Ladies, her arms full of toilet rolls. "Just in case," she muttered, defensively. "You never know when the floodgates are going to open."

Out in the car park, I stepped over a squirming, squealing Mum as Biffa sat astride her, pinning her to the tarmac. My bike was behind the bins, its tyres intact but the pedals had vanished. "Oh dear!" exclaimed Freckly Girl. "Who's done that? My bike looks alright, thank goodness; I can give you a doubler."

I straddled her rear rack and she started to pedal. Although she was slender, she was very athletic and we whizzed along the roads, which were beginning to turn frosty. A fire engine shot past us in the opposite direction, sirens blaring. We stopped at Den's Diner and Freckly Girl bought me a bag of chips, although I didn't feel much like eating. When we arrived home, I stopped her from cycling into the drive. "You never know what's lying in wait for you."

"Oh. Right."

I hopped off the back of the bike. "Thank you, er, Freck, er, I mean-"

She smiled. "It's Bonnie."

"What is?"

"My name."

"Ah. Thank you, Bonnie. You've been very kind."

She manoeuvred her bicycle around then turned to look at me. "Morten, I was wondering, just on the off-chance, that is, and I know the timing's not very good, but I've got two tickets to see Katy Perry at the O2 in January. Would you like to go?"

I gaped at her, the full moon making her face even paler. "See Katy? You mean, in real life?"

"Yes. I heard she's brilliant live." She bit her lip nervously. "Unless you don't want to, of course."

"I'd love to!" I burst out. "I'd love to see Katy! It would be a dream come true, but I don't know who I could give the other ticket to now Myra and I are not, well, you know. I suppose I could ask my mate Barry, he's always said he'd like to do Katy-"

"Morten, when I said I had two tickets I was hoping we could go together. You and me. As in, a date." Bonnie's face was now the same colour as her hair.

"Oh!" Freckly Bonnie was asking me out! I was almost too surprised to speak. "I see. A date - with me? Are you absolutely sure? Well, yes, that would be very nice."

"Great!" she looked relieved. "I'll give you a call then, shall I?"

I nodded vigorously. She leant over and kissed me on the cheek. "Night then, Morten."

"Good night Bon-" her lips were locked on mine; blimey! She tasted of lovely greasy chips and she was an extremely gentle kisser - she didn't even try to force her tongue into my mouth or grip my ears in her fists, like Myra did. I didn't want the moment to end.

When she finally pulled away, she smiled a beautiful smile right into my eyes. "See you then," she whispered, and cycled away. I watched her go, wanting to run after her but my legs felt rather weak all of a sudden. I should have asked her in for a glass of strawberry Nesquik, but perhaps that would have been a bit too forward. I'd ask her in next time, or when we got back from seeing Katy. From seeing Katy! She might well recognise me in the crowd - she should do, I'd tweeted her at least one hundred and twenty pictures of myself.

I gazed up at the magical starry sky, finding myself humming "I kissed a girl and I liked it", then forced my wobbly legs to carry me up the drive. A demonic cackle rang out and something thudded against my chest and slid down the front of my trousers; a turkey carcass. I hardly noticed.

I sat at the kitchen table, poured myself a glass of milk and wrote a letter.

Dear Peanut

I am sorry that I am not going to be your Dad after all. But even though I feel so very sad, it gladdens my heart to know that there are so many men in Shodsworth who want to be your father, and they are even prepared to fight for the honour! So you see, you really are the luckiest Peanut alive - to be wanted is the best feeling in the world.

Even though, after the DNA testing, you will soon have a proper Dad, I want you to know that I will always be here for you. If you ever need someone for advice on relationships, or cycling proficiency, or pet insurance, you can come to me. I often wish I could talk to my Dad, man to man, but he's an extremely busy entrepreneur and hasn't got round to buying a phone yet. I write to him though, and often talk to him at night, when I'm in bed. I've told him all about you; he can't hear me, of course, but I live with the hope that one day he'll return to Shodsworth. I know that rumour about a lynch mob is just a silly joke!

I hope I will have Peanuts of my own someday - maybe you will all play together! Wouldn't that be wonderful? I know my mother isn't keen on having red-haired grandchildren (when I was being born she shrieked at the midwife: "if it's a ginger stick it back up there") but I've got the feeling my own little Peanuts may well have a few freckles! I can't say any more than that, but we'll have a chat about these things when you're old enough!

I've got to go now Peanut, but remember that I loved you and wanted you so very, very much.

Love

Morten aka Foggy

PS

Ask your Dad to take you to watch the cars on the Shodsworth flyover as soon as you're old enough - I think I was about four when my father first left me there for the day. It's just brilliant!

--The End--

Also by Jo Edwards

You can catch up on all the action at Perypils Insurance in Jo's best selling novel, **Work Wife Balance** and its sequel, **Pot-bound**.

WORK WIFE BALANCE

Kate King is flailing to keep afloat. As her team bicker, finger-point and cheat their way through rumours of sackings and site closures, her ill-tempered husband is becoming increasingly embittered and secretive.

If things aren't bad enough, Kate also has to contend with a career-climbing, attractive younger colleague and the sudden appearance of back fat.

Something has to give, but will it be her marriage or her job? And which does she care about more?

"Kate is a wonderful character, believable, likeable and with a nice line in funny put-downs. This is well-written, very funny and I raced through it, occasionally squealing in horror at the antics of Kate's colleagues. It's also a joy to read about a strong woman with a big job and fiery opinions, a nice antidote to the sugary sweet sort of chick lit." Daily Mail

"Best book in a long time! I have never read a book where I have laughed out loud before. Not the sort of book you can read quietly in bed next to a snoring husband! I felt that by the end of the book Kate was a friend not a character from a book. Funny funny book, can't wait to start on Pot Bound." Amazon Reviewer

POT-BOUND

"The roots of a pot-bound plant wind themselves round and round the inside of the pot making an impenetrable wall."

Skiving colleagues, hideous bosses, outrageous friends - will Kate be capable of laying new roots amidst the harshness and turbulence of her life, or will she forever be twisted around into knots?

"A fantastic follow up to Work Wife Balance. Didn't think Kate's life could get much funnier and complicated but this was a real gem!"

"It's good to find a book with a strong female lead that has a real job and a real life. Got strange looks on the plane from laughing out loud so much."

FOGGY'S BLOG

I am Morten Astley Fogarty, call centre worker and all-round entertainer. Although I have an extremely rewarding career answering the phones at Perypils Insurance (customers are always telling me what a total brick I am), my ambition is to perform on the stage. I am, after all, named after two of the greatest singers of the 1980's.

My girlfriend has a fantastic voice too and we often duet together. She has asked me to consider a three-way, so if I can find the right person to perform with us, we might even become the next Earth, Wind and Fire!

YOURS, EUNICE

Help is at hand! Agony Aunt extraordinaire, Eunice Peaks, answers your letters and offers sound, practical advice on family, relationships, work and container gardening – a problem shared is a problem halved!

"Dear Brenda

How awful for you! Both parents terminally ill – what a dreadful bind. I do so understand the crippling guilt that you describe in your letter; you feel you should be doing so much more to help them. What a shame your husband's left you, and obviously you no longer have the support of your best friend now; I hope she makes a full recovery from that mysterious hit and run incident.

Well, do try and keep your spirits up. I think a break would do you the world of good. Maybe you could take a nice long holiday – Australia, perhaps? They have a wonderful Girl Guides following out there and I've taken the liberty of enclosing some contact details for Joyce who runs the Darwin chapter. There won't be any accommodation fees as long as you help her herd the cattle, and there might be a little light kangaroo culling to undertake but just think - by the time you get back to your parents, the worst should all be over! Won't that be a relief? Have a wonderful time.

Yours, Eunice."

Visit www.jo-edwards.com to read more of Eunice's inimitable responses.

ABOUT THE AUTHOR

Author Photograph Siân Edwards
© Richard Edwards Photography

Jo Edwards lives and works in Hampshire, in the UK. Her debut novel, Work Wife Balance, became an Amazon bestseller and its sequel, Pot-bound, was released in May 2013. A Very Foggy Christmas is the follow-up novella to Foggy's Blog.

Jo is always delighted to hear from readers – please do visit her at: www.jo-edwards.com

For more information and links:

Other Weasel Green Press paperbacks:

Dulcie Feenan:
Christmas comes to Oddleton

J.A. Clement:
On Dark Shores series
    1: The Lady & 2: The Other Nereia

Other Weasel Green Press e-books:

Dulcie Feenan:
Christmas comes to Oddleton

J.A. Clement:
On Dark Shores series
    1: The Lady & 2: The Other Nereia

Parallels series:

The Black-Eyed Susan

Flight from Shantar

Song of the Ice Lord

A Sprig of Holly

Printed in Great Britain
by Amazon